David Roberts

D1235744

THE HOLY LAN[

David Roberts was born in ~~Stockbridge, Edinburg~~ He was apprenticed for seven years to a painter and decorator, during which time he studied art in the evenings. Roberts started work as a professional scene painter at the Theatre Royal, Edinburgh in 1822. In the same year, he showed three of his architectural pictures in the Exhibition of Living Artists. Soon he moved to London to the sceneroom of Covent Garden.

After his first trip to the Continent, his reputation was made when he exhibited his collection of drawings. By 1826 he was able to leave the theatrical world, and concentrate on art, selling and exhibiting his works, until in 1831 he was elected President of the Society of British Artists.

Several years later he made an extended journey to the Middle East — sketching and painting. He became sick with "intermittent fever", thought to have been brought on by the severe privations that he endured during his journeys. On his return to England, his drawings created a sensation. The originality of the places he had discovered caused great excitement and widespread interest in the world of art of his day. He became an R.A. in 1841 and was honoured with the Freedom of the City of Edinburgh in 1858.

During his lifetime he painted some 260 oil paintings — many of which can be seen today in the London Museums. He died in 1864 and is buried in Norward cemetery.

Jerusalem – The Old City (Jerusalem from the South)

Jerusalem lies near the summit of a broad mountain ridge. It was founded in the forty-sixth year of Abraham, 2177 years before the siege of Titus. It was even then named Salem (Peace), doubtless with prophetic reference to its future purposes, as the centre of pure religion in the world.

Jerusalem – Site of the Temple

"This fine monument, the Mosque of Omar, stands on Mount Moriah, the ancient site of the Temple." For many hundreds of years pilgrims have come to this Holy Place in Jerusalem regarded as the centre of the world. "The group consists of Greek Christians praying towards the Holy Sepulchre. They stand on a terrace of the dilapidated Church of St. Anna. The Mount of Olives is partially seen to the left."

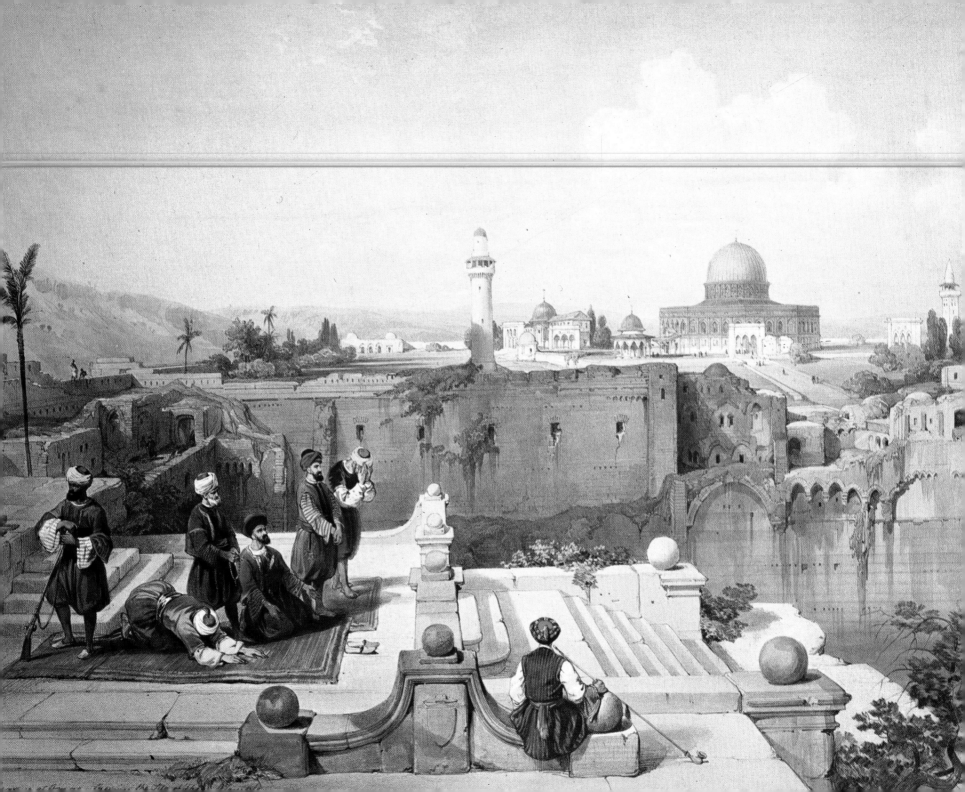

Jerusalem – The Holy Sepulchre (The Exterior of the Holy Sepulchre)
"The first and most interesting object within the walls of the Holy City, the spot to which every pilgrim directs his steps, is the Holy Sepulchre: but the traveller finds his expectation strangely disappointed when, approaching the hallowed tomb, he sees around him the tottering houses of a ruined city, and is conducted to the door of a gigantic church"..."The ruined tower to the left was anciently the belfry."

The Citadel (The Tower of David)
The Citadel of modern Jerusalem, an irregular assemblage of square towers, lies on the north-western part of Sion, to the South of the Jaffa Gate. A sloping bulwark protects the towers, and bears evident marks of remote antiquity — it is thought by Robinson to be of the time of Hadrian. Some of the stones of the north-eastern tower are 12 feet long by 3 feet 5 inches broad.

Golden Gate of the Temple
Shewing part of the
ancient walls

The Pool of Siloah (The Upper Fountain of Siloah)

Siloam consists of two basins or fountains, the upper one of which is a fissure in the solid rock. A flight of steps leads down on the inside to the water, and close at hand, on the outside is the reservoir. This seems to be generally acknowledged as ''Siloa's brook that flowed fast by the oracle of God''. The drawing of the water from Siloam in the Feast of Tabernacles became a remarkable ceremonial in the latter ages of Judea.

Jerusalem – The Golden Gate

This is a massive structure — a double gateway. After the second revolt A.D. 136, Hadrian built a new city Aelia, and raised a temple to Jupiter. The style of the Golden Gate refers it to this period. The external front and arches are of Roman origin; and of the interior it is evident that ''a central row of noble Corinthian columns and a groined roof, had once formed a stately portico of Roman workmanship.''

Jerusalem – The Old City (View from the Mount of Olives)
"....legend has largely usurped the place of history; but nature remains: all the great featues of the scene are unchangeable; and he who now explores the valleys or climbs the hills of this illustrious region is secure that there at least he cannot be deceived. Every outline of those hills, every undulation of those valleys has the matchless influence of reality — he looks on the landscape where the great agents of Providence gazed . . . ."

Jerusalem – Damascus Gate
"The walls of Jerusalem are chiefly modern and Saracenic, but are built evidently on the site of more ancient walls, raised in the time of the Crusaders, and those, not improbably, formed of the material of others still more ancient." The Damascus Gate built by the Sultan Suleiman the Magnificent in the sixteenth century looks to the North. Camels were the main form of transport, and there was a constant stream of traffic on this great northern highway leading to Nablus and Damascus.

Bethlehem – The Shrine of the Nativity

"This chamber, partly an excavation in the limestone, lies directly under the Church built by Queen Helena.... On the right are three lamps suspended over the Manger....opposite this the altar....said by the monks to mark the place where the Magi knelt to make their offerings. On the left is a semicircular recess, a glory represents the Star which guided the Magi."

Bethlehem

"....the village lies about two hours distance from Jerusalem. The surrounding country — though hilly, is fertile and well-cultivated. In the distance are seen the hills of Moab, and below them a glimpse of the Dead Sea. In the interval between the Greek Convent and the mountain border of the Dead Sea rises a hill, named the Hill of the Franks, from a legend of the Crusades."

The Wilderness of Ein Gedi and the Convent of Mar Saba

"The Convent of St. Saba is about four leagues to the south east of Jerusalem. The surrounding country is desert. The entrance doors are low, narrow and formed of iron or very thick wood. The Monks pay and keep a regular guard of Arabs at the principal entrance; and in one of the towers a sentinel is constantly posted, to announce the approach of travellers or of Bedouins."

Hebron

Hebron is one of the most memorable sites of Palestine. It is one of the most ancient cities in the world, built "seven years before Zoar in Egypt". The Artist describes Hebron: "On turning the side of a hill, the little town of Hebron burst upon us.... Its situation is beautiful, and the houses glittering in the noon-day sun had a look of English cleanliness after the wretched hovels of Egypt. The children who came out to meet us were among the most beautiful I had ever seen. The countenance was truly Jewish, but with a healthy rosy colour which I have seldom seen out of England."

Jericho — (Encampment of the Pilgrims at Jericho)

At Easter the neighbourhood of Jericho is frequented by Pilgrims who come to purify themselves in the River Jordan. But the land retains its ancient character for lawlessness, and the devotees are escorted by a strong military force under the direction of the Governor of Jerusalem.

The principal object in the engraving is the tent of the Governor, Achmed Aga, who invited the Artist to accompany him to the Jordan (April 1839). The scene was strikingly oriental . . . .pilgrims of all costumes, officers of the escort galloping in all directions . . .some throwing the djerid, others firing at marks, groups of men, women and children, some at rest, some in sport, and some in prayer, the whole illuminated by a sunset of remarkable vividness.

The River Jordan — (The Immersion of the Pilgrims)

"In this view, Achmed Aga, the governor of Jerusalem, with part of his Arab guard occupy the foreground.... As we approached the brink of the River, a general rush took place...even the camels, though heavily loaded, could scarcely be restrained. The Governor's carpets were spread on a high bank close to the River, where we could command a view of the entire scene; the military band and colours were brought round him and seats were assigned to our party. One of the achievements is to be the first to plunge into the stream.''

Nablus (The Tomb of Joseph at Shechem)

"Among the relics associated with Biblical history at Nablous, the tomb of Joseph is an object of great veneration. The tomb is plain, and plastered over, with a small recess at the foot, in which some small lamps were placed, probably by pious Jews. The people hold this spot in deep reverence."

Sebaste – Ancient Samaria

"....Sebaste was founded by Omri, King of Israel, about the year 925 B.C. Samaria continued, during the centuries, to be the chief city of the ten tribes, and during the whole period it was the seat of idolatry. The vast ruins which now exist at Sebaste are chiefly those of the Palace of Herod....who enriched Samaria with splendid edifices.... Such appears to have been the Samaria of the New Testament, in which Philip preached the Gospel, and where a church was formed by the Apostles."

Nazareth – The Church of the Annunciation

The Church is a lofty nave, with three elevations. The columns and whole interior of the building are hung with damasked striped silk, which gives it a glowing appearance. "Finding the door of the Church open we went in; it was the hour of vespers, and the chanting of the monks, sustained by the mellow tones of the organ, which came upon us unexpectedly, was solemn and affecting. The interior is small and plain, with massive arches, the hangings of the walls produced a rich effect, the whole impression transported me back to Italy."

Nazareth — Convent of the Terra Sancta

The site of Nazareth is admirable: and in the days when the land was fully peopled . . . .the valley of Nazareth may have been one of the loveliest spots in Palestine. Richardson describes it, "as if fifteen mountains met to form an enclosure for this delightful spot: . . .a rich and beautiful field in the midst of barren hills; it abounds in fig trees, small gardens and hedges of the prickly pear . . . ." The village stands on the slope of the west side of the valley, the Convent at the east end on high ground. In the village there is but one Mosque, which, however, forms a prominent feature in the view.

Mount Tabor (from the Plain of Estraelon)

Tabor is a beautiful mountain, wholly of limestone, and rising about a thousand feet above the great Plain of Estraelon. "The present view", observes the Artist, "was taken while crossing the Plain, on the road from Jenin to Nazareth". The figures in the foreground are a Caravan of Christian pilgrims whom the Artist found resting during the mid-day on their return from Damascus to Jerusalem.

Cana of Galilee

The view is full of traditionary holiness. In the small Greek Church at the foot of the hill, is shewn by the priest, as an invaluable relic (on the authority of tradition) "one of the water pots" in which the water was changed into wine. For preservation it is built into the wall. The Church itself is pronounced to have been raised on the spot where the marriage feast was celebrated.

Tiberias (from the Walls)

This sketch, in addition to the view of the City, gives in the distance, crowning a lofty hill, the City of Safed. The land is peculiarly liable to earthquakes. Safed was fearfully visited in the middle of the last century (1759): but a still heavier visitation befell it in 1837. Safed is venerated as one of the four holy cities of Judea, the others being Jerusalem, Hebron and Tiberias.

Tiberias on the Sea of Galilee (looking towards Hermon)

The ancient city of Tiberias, built by Herod Antipas, has long since perished. Herod compelled a population from the surrounding provinces to fill his City, adorned it with structures, of which the very fragments are stately; gave it peculiar priveleges; and building a palace, which was one of the wonders of the land, declared Tiberias the Capital of Galilee. The ruins in the sketch are those of the modern City prostrated by the earthquake. The view commands various sites memorable from their connexion with the Scriptures . . . . in the horizon is the majestic Hermon 10.000 feet above the Mediterranean.

Galilee
1839

The Sea of Galilee (The Sea of Tiberias looking towards Bashan)

The dimensions of the Lake are variously stated by travellers.... Myriads of birds resort to its shores. Its water is cool and clear, and abounds with fish. The Artist gives his personal impression of the scene: "Passing through a beautiful country, in about five hours we came in sight of the Sea of Galilee, embosomed in surrounding hills; far on the left lay Mount Hermon, covered with snow, and on a nearer hill rests the City of Safed.... Towards the West the River Jordan was seen flowing from the Lake towards the Dead Sea, and below us lay the Town of Tiberias."

The Valley of the Jordan and the Dead Sea

"The view when we emerged from the rocky hills was one not to be forgotten. The Valley of the Jordan lay stretched beneath our feet, in all the beauty of an Eastern evening. The Dead Sea, the silvery line of the rapid Jordan just visible, the gay colours of the pilgrims' encampment glittering in the latest rays of the setting sun, were fitter for the poet than the painter."

Roberts. R.A.   St Jean d'Acre

Haifa, Mt. Carmel (Caiphas — looking toward Mt. Carmel)
This view is taken from near the mouth of the River Kishon, and in the foreground characteristically lies one of the wrecks which constantly strew this exposed shore . . . . On the left is seen the summit of Mt. Tabor, with portions of the Lesser Hermon and Gilboa, and the opposite Mountain of Samaria. The eye then rests on the long line of Carmel, with the "Convent of Elias" on its summit, and the town of Caipha glittering at its foot. A succession of mountain ridges stretch from East to West: and to the right is a "sea of hills", surmounted by Hermon, with its icy crown."

(St Jean d'Acre.) Acre
"This view gives the sea face of Acre, exhibiting a striking succession of domes, minarets, and that general style of ornamental building which is so attractive to the eye at a distance, but which so frequently disappoints it on a nearer view. Still the Oriental architecture has a charm of its own . . . .combining all that was romantic in the East, with all that was superb . . . ."

Ancient Ashdod

"Ashdod of the Old Testament, Azotus of the New, and Asdood of the present day, stands about ten miles from Jaffa. It is now but a wretched village, though its position in the midst of a fertile country, and commanding a portion of the route along the coast, may yet restore it to some share of its early importance." In the Jewish annals it is distinguished as one of the Five Chief Cities of the Philistines. Ashdod was the City to which the captive Ark was brought after the defeat of the Israelite army.

Ancient Jaffa – looking South

"Jaffa . . . . rose into early importance as the chief harbour of Judaea. Like all eastern cities the interior disappoints the eye. Narrow streets loaded with mire in winter, and choked with dust in the summer, a struggling population compressed into hovels which seem the natural nests of disease . . . . A Greek, a Latin and an Armenian Convent constitute the town and its people. It was the nearest port to the Holy City . . . . The figures in the foreground are Polish Jews returning from their pilgrimage to Jerusalem and waiting for embarkation."

The Coral Island (Island of Graia)

Traditionally the Beni–sa′id Arabs believe that a great City once existed on the Island with a magnificent harbour . . .now not a solitary sail is ever seen. The waters teem with fish, but only one man was seen at Akabah pursuing fishing as an employment: he caught a great number of excellent fish, and supplied the Caravan of the Artist's party with a great treat after the fare of the Desert. The form of the Island and its ruins, backed by the distant range of mountains, and the effect under which they are represented, give great beauty to this highly picturesque subject.

Monastery of St. Katherine

This scene represents the arrival of the Caravan of the Artist and his companions. The Mountain is red granite, without a trace of vegetation, and rises majestically to the height of 5,000 feet. The Monastery has been built in the form of a square fortress of hewn granite, and flanked with towers...its strength forms the chief security of the inhabitants; for it is accessible only by a projecting trap door. The Monastery is large and resembles a small town, containing many buildings, several courts and storehouses, a Mosque with a minaret, and a Chapel.